YOUR KNOWLEDGE HAS VALUE

Bibliographic information published by the German National Library:

The German National Library lists this publication in the National Bibliography; detailed bibliographic data are available on the Internet at http://dnb.dnb.de .

Imprint:

Copyright © 2019 GRIN Verlag
Print and binding: Books on Demand GmbH, Norderstedt Germany
ISBN: 9783346109996

This book at GRIN:

https://www.grin.com/document/512540

Fatima Tariq

Blasphemy laws in Pakistan

Case Study of Mst. Asia Bibi v The State

GRIN Verlag

GRIN - Your knowledge has value

Since its foundation in 1998, GRIN has specialized in publishing academic texts by students, college teachers and other academics as e-book and printed book. The website www.grin.com is an ideal platform for presenting term papers, final papers, scientific essays, dissertations and specialist books.

Visit us on the internet:

http://www.grin.com/

http://www.facebook.com/grincom

http://www.twitter.com/grin_com

BLASPHEMY LAWS IN PAKISTAN

Part I: INTRODUCTION

WHAT IS BLASPHEMY?

For many people, one of the most fearful terms to be found in the New Testament is the word "blasphemy."[1] Blasphemy is represented as a horrible sin, but what is it? Have I been guilty of it? Can one obtain pardon for it? These are serious questions that engage the attention of the religious person. Blasphemy is derived from the Greek term *blasphemia*, which scholars believe probably derives from two words: *bapto* : to injure, and pheme, to speak. The word would thus suggest "injurious speech."[2] Blasphemy is the act of insulting or showing disrespect or lack of esteem to a deity, to religious or holy persons or sacred things, or toward something considered sacred or inviolable.[3]

BLASPHEMY LAWS

Blasphemy law is a law limiting the freedom of speech and expression relating to blasphemy, or irreverence toward holy personages, religious history, customs, or beliefs.[4] Blasphemy laws are sometimes used to protect the religious beliefs of a majority, while in other cases, they serve to offer protection of the religious beliefs of minorities. Different countries have different laws on the offense of blasphemy under their constitutions and sometimes under divine law.[5]

---

1 https://www.christiancourier.com/articles/168-blasphemy-what-is-this-great-sin

2 Hewett, Bob. 2002

3 Miriam Díez Bosch and Jordi Sànchez Torrents (2015). *On blasphemy*. Barcelona: Blanquerna Observatory on Media, Religion and Culture.

4 https://nation.com.pk/28-Sep-2018/freedom-of-speech-and-blasphemy

5 https://www.refworld.org/docid/3ae6a9aa4.html

HISTORICAL OVERVIEW

In 1860 British introduced three blasphemy laws in Indian penal code i.e. 295, 296 and 298 and the fourth blasphemy law was enacted in 1927 which was known as section 295-A.[6] Pakistan adopted the same four laws and different amendment few made at a later stage in terms of punishments. Out of these aforementioned three sections, this paper will merely discussing the section 295, 295A and further discuss 295-B and 295C which was enacted during the government of gen Zia ul Haq.

SECTION 295-B & 295-C

Zia ul Haq introduced 295-B and 295-C in the penal code in 1982 and in 1986 respectively. 295-B states that " Defiling, etc. of copy of Holy Qur'an. Whoever willfully defiles damages or desecrates a copy of the Holy Qur'an or of an extract therefrom or uses it in any derogatory manner or for any unlawful purpose shall be punishable with imprisonment for life."[7] While 295-C states that, "Use of derogatory remarks, etc. in respect of the Holy Prophet. Whoever by words, either spoken or written, or by visible representation, or by any imputation, innuendo, or insinuation, directly or indirectly, defiles the sacred name of the Holy Prophet (peace be upon him) shall be punished with death, or imprisonment for life, and shall also be liable to a fine." [8]

Contrary to the blasphemy laws enacted by the British government that addressed to all the religious beliefs, the new laws were specific to the Islam, even in some cases these laws were made for some specific sect of Islam. In the case of 295-B it addressed the issue of defiling a copy of Holy Quran. It specifically protects the sanctity of Holy Quran but there is no law to protect non-Muslims from any act which may hurt their religious feelings. The enactment of these laws led to increase in blasphemy cases. There were only seven

---

6 https://blogs.tribune.com.pk/story/3270/where-did-the-blasphemy-law-come-from/

7Section 295-B, PPC

8 Section 295-C, PPC

blasphemy cases from 1851 to 1947 and after enactment of these new blasphemy laws in 1977, there were 80 blasphemy cases during the Zia's rule (1977-1988).[9]

Part II: CASE STUDY

Mst. Asia Bibi v The State

(Crl.A. No.39-L of 2015)

FACTS AND JUDGMENT

The facts of the case are that on 14 June 2009, Asia Bibi allegedly uttered derogatory remarks against the Holy Prophet Muhammad (Peace Be Upon Him) and the Holy Qur'an, while she was plucking *falsa* (purple berries) along with other Muslim ladies in the fields of one Muhammad Idrees in village Ittanwali, District Nankana, the Province of Punjab. Two Muslim ladies, namely, Mafia Bibi and Asma Bibi, narrated this incidence to the complainant, Qari Muhammad Salaam. On 19 June 2009, he called the accused to a public gathering, where she allegedly confessed her guilt, and on the same day a First Information Report (FIR) was registered against Asia Bibi under section 295-C of the PPC at the Police Station Sadar, District Nankana.

The prosecution's case was essentially premised on the statements of the eyewitnesses and the alleged extra-judicial confession. Asia Bibi, however, denied the allegations. In the statement under section 342 of the Code of Criminal Procedure 1898 ('CrPC'), she stated, "…I have great respect and honor to the Holy Prophet (PBUH) as well as Holy Quran and since police have conspired with the complainant, so, the police have falsely booked me in this case…."[10]

---

9 Nafees, Mohammad. "Blasphemy Laws in Pakistan A Historical Overview." 2014

10 Mst. Asia Bibi v The State Crl.A. No.39-L of 2015, paragraph [28]

The trial court convicted Asia Bibi under section 295-C of the PPC vide judgment dated 8 November 2010 and sentenced her to death with a fine of Rs.1,00,000. In default of payment, thereof, she was liable to undergo simple imprisonment for a period of six months. Asia Bibi appealed against her conviction before the LHC,[11] which dismissed this appeal, vide judgment dated 16 October 2014. In appeal against this judgment, the SC reappraised the evidence on the record and acquitted Asia Bibi after finding her innocent because the prosecution failed to prove guilt beyond a reasonable doubt.

CRITICAL ANALYSIS

The three-judge bench which acquitted Asia Bibi comprised the sitting chief justice, Justice Saqib Nisar, and Justice Asif Khosa.

The first 11 pages of the main 34-page judgment, penned by ex Chief Justice Nisar, read like a tutorial: what constitutes blasphemy; why it ought to be punished with death; why Pakistan incorporated laws to punish blasphemy; and how Pakistan inspired the 2009 United Nations resolution that declared defamation of religion as a violation of human rights.

It quotes copiously from the Quran and the Prophet's tradition to establish sanctity. But it then goes on to discuss "another aspect of the matter," which is that "sometimes, to fulfil nefarious designs, the law is misused by individuals levelling false allegations of blasphemy".[12]

It says 62 people have been killed for blasphemy since 1990 "even before their trial could be conducted in accordance with the law", and mentions **the lynching of Mashal Khan at Mardan University** as the latest example.[13]

The order also underlines the Prophet's attitude towards other religions.

---

11 Criminal Appeal No. 2509 of 2010, which was heard along with Murder Reference No. 614 of 2010.

12 https://www.bbc.com/news/world-asia-46048134

13 https://www.euronews.com/2017/04/14/pakistan-blasphemy-killing-murdered-student-devoted-to-islam

In a separate 21-page note penned by Justice Khosa, he quotes from what is known as St Katherine's Covenant to establish how the Prophet guaranteed protection to Christians in the Islamic state. Justice Khosa runs a greater risk than Chief Justice Nisar. He headed the bench which in 2015 upheld the death sentence of **Mumtaz Qadri**, the self-confessed killer of Punjab Governor Salman Taseer. Qadri was hanged in February 2016.[14]

After killing Taseer, Qadri became a hero of the anti-blasphemy lobby. After his death, he was given the burial of a saint in his village near Islamabad. A mausoleum has since been built over his grave where devotees flock to pray and make offerings.[15]

For anti-blasphemy leaders, Asia Bibi's case offered the court a chance to make up for his hanging by letting her hang too. Apart from offering a quid pro quo, this would have turned Asia Bibi into a legally sanctioned example of what would happen when someone is accused of blasphemy the next time.

PRESUMPTION OF INNOCENCE

There is a Latin expression: *Ei incumbet probatio qui dicit, non qui negat.* It means that "the burden of proof is upon the one who declares, not upon one who denies."[16] The prosecution is required to prove every element of a crime, including the requisite criminal intent (mens rea) in order to convict a defendant. This is behind the principle that a person is considered **innocent unless proven guilty.**[17]

Most systems of law agree with this principle, including the Islamic jurisprudence. In fact under the Islamic concept of justice even casting suspicion on a person is highly condemned as per hadith documented by Bukhari and Muslim. Hazrat Ali has also been cited as saying, *Avert the prescribed punishment by rejecting doubtful evidence*.[18] The UN's

---

14 PLD 2016 SC 17.

15 https://www.bbc.com/news/world-asia-46048134

16https://www.pakistantoday.com.pk/2017/11/27/what-happened-to-innocent-until-proven-guilty/

17 http://legalhistorysources.com/Law508/InnocentGuilty.htm

18https://www.pakistantoday.com.pk/2017/11/27/what-happened-to-innocent-until-proven-guilty/

Universal Declaration of Human Rights also incorporates this principle as do civilian codes of law in many countries. Constitution of Pakistan also guarantees these rights. **Article: 10A** is wholly talk about Right to a fair trial.[19]

VIOLATION OF RIGHTS

How Blasphemy Laws Cause Infringement Of Fundamental Rights

Courts hearing Section 295-C cases however, have not required proof of intent beyond a reasonable doubt in order to convict a person of the offence.[20] This is true even though the Federal Shariat Court in 1990 ruled that blasphemy under section 295-C was an "intentional or reckless wrong", in which the mens rea amounts to "intention, purpose, design, or at least foresight."[21] The conviction of an individual in the absence of proof beyond a reasonable doubt of all elements of a crime, including the requisite intent, would violate the presumption of innocence and consequently the right to a fair trial.

Asiya Bibi Case: Asia bibi was arrested in June 2009 on charges of blasphemy. She was held in pre-trial detention for over sixteen months before a trial court found her guilty in November 2010 and sentenced her to death. She appealed to the Lahore High Court, and it took nearly another four years for her appeal to be decided. In November 2014, Asia bibi appealed to the Supreme Court, and it took a further eight months for the Supreme Court just to admit her case for hearing. By any standard, this period of time, all of which was spent in custody violates her right to be tried within a reasonable time.

Asia bibi's case is not an exception. The average time between arrest and trial in blasphemy cases is between two to three years. In many cases, the accused is not granted bail, and thus is held in custody throughout this pretrial period, implicating their rights not

---

19 https://pakistanconstitutionlaw.com/article-10a-right-to-fair-trial/

20 Mirza Mubarak Ahmed v. State, 1989 MLD 896, p. 898

21 PLD 1991 Federal Shariat Court 10.

only to trial within a reasonable time, but also the rights to liberty and the presumption of innocence.

Wajih-ul-Hassan v. The State: At the end of September, the Supreme Court acquitted a man who had been condemned to death in a blasphemy case in 2002 and had consequently remained behind bars for 18 years.[22] Wajih-ul-Hassan has spent over 17 years in prison mere on allegations.

A case was registered against Hassan in 1999 for writing blasphemous letters to a lawyer. In 2001, a handwriting expert in his report said that the writing of the accused closely matched with the letters in question, following which the trial court convicted Hassan and awarded him death sentence.[23] The decision was later maintained by the Lahore High Court as well.[24]

From the study of the above cases, it is *prima facie* that blasphemy laws cause violations of rights to equality and equal protection of law as well as due process and fair trial through the failure of administrative and judicial organs of the state.

Part III: FLAWS IN LAW

The most controversial section which is often misused is section 295-C, which addressed the use of derogatory remarks in respect of Holy Prophet(SAW). Essentially the punishment for committing this offence was either imprisonment for life or death sentence. But in 1991, the Federal Shariat Court of Pakistan struck down the punishment of life imprisonment and made <u>death penalty</u> mandatory in ***Muhammad Ismail Qureshi versus Federation of Pakistan***.[25]

22https://www.ndtv.com/world-news/pakistan-supreme-court-releases-man-sentenced-to-death-after-18-years-says-no-evidence-no-witness-2107600

23http://www.humanrights.asia/news/urgent-appeals/UA-35-2002/

24 Wajih-ul-Hassan v. Ismail Qureshi, 2010, Lahore High Court (unreported).

25 P L D 1991 Federal Shariat Court 10

LACK OF INTENT

A very important flaw in the drafting of this provision is that it does not take into account of *intention of an offender*. The word intentionally/willfully/deliberately is missing from this provision which make its problematic. Without the determination of mens rea state is prosecuting a person and giving him a death sentence while he or she does not have any intention to commit crime. While unintentional and intentional offences are treated in the same way by giving the same punishment for both offences. The example of ***Younus Sheikh vs. State*** gives the clear picture of this procedural flaw.[26] Mohammed Younus Shaikh was a medical doctor, human rights activist and freethinker, and he was accused of blasphemy and he was charged by the court ordered to pay a fine of 100,000 rupees, and sentenced him to death by hanging and later acquitted. Shaikh's blasphemy was alleged to have occurred at a lecture which he allegedly delivered on 2nd of October, 2000, in Capital Medical College. In this way, it was said that, during the lecture, Shaikh said that Muhammad did not become a Muslim until the age of 40 (the age at which the Prophet is believed to receive his first revelation). Moreover, it was also said that he talked about Prophet's parents and called them non-Muslims by saying that had already died before Islam even came into existence. Furthermore, he is known to say that the Prophet married at the age of 25 and that it was not an Islamic marriage contract. He also talked about other things such as circumcision, shaving, etc. and said that those practices were unknown to his tribe. However, these things were allegedly said while answering the question regarding the practices of Arab before Islam.[27] The response was just an answer to question and no mens rea or malicious intent was there in the statements thus this case was the perfect example of misuse of section 295-C.

---

26 https://www.theguardian.com/world/2001/aug/20/rorymccarthy

27 Siddique, Osama, and Zahra Hayat. "Unholy Speech and Holy Laws: Blasphemy Laws in Pakistan." MINNESOTA JOURNAL OF INTERNATIONAL LAW

The lack of intent in section 295 even makes a room for courts to prosecute mentally deranged and retarded person against blasphemy. It can be seen in the case of **Arshad Javed** who was convicted under section 295C and Additional Sessions Judge, Bahawalpur sentenced him to death.[28]

UNJUSTIFIABLE PUNISHMENT: A COMPARISON WITH OTHER MUSLIM COUNTRIES

Section 295-C of the Pakistan Penal Code provides death sentence or imprisonment for life and offender shall also be liable to pay a fine. While in **_Bangladesh_**, the maximum punishment for committing blasphemy is imprisonment of two years, or fine, or both. Article 513 of **_Iran's penal code_** provides maximum imprisonment of five years for committing blasphemy against Holy Prophet PBUH. **_Indonesian penal code_** provides the maximum punishment of 5 years in prison for committing blasphemy. So the comparison clearly shows that Pakistan is the only country which provides death sentence for committing blasphemy.

Part IV: MISUSE OF BLASPHEMY LAWS

i.   Used for suppressing minorities

Zia ul Haq and his supporters made these laws to differentiate Islam from other religions and to provide a legal procedure to address Islamic issues but the outcome of these laws was totally opposite and highly problematic. They are used against religious minorities in most of the cases and in some cases these laws are used against Muslims who have different sect. One can conclude that these laws were made to protect a single sect which is in majority in multi-religious society. Zia himself was a deobandi and these laws clearly reflect the prejudice towards deobandi. Soon after the enactment of these laws there was a sudden rise in the blasphemy cases and many innocent people have been falsely accused under these laws.

28State v. Muhammad Arshad Javed, (1995) 13 M.L.D. 667, 669 (Lahore)

According to a report, from 1953 to July 2012, there were **434** convictions under blasphemy laws and there were _258 Muslims, 114 Christians, 57 Ahmadis_ and _4 Hindus_. The convictions are increasing day by day. The latest research by the _Center for Social Justice_ shows following statistics:[29]

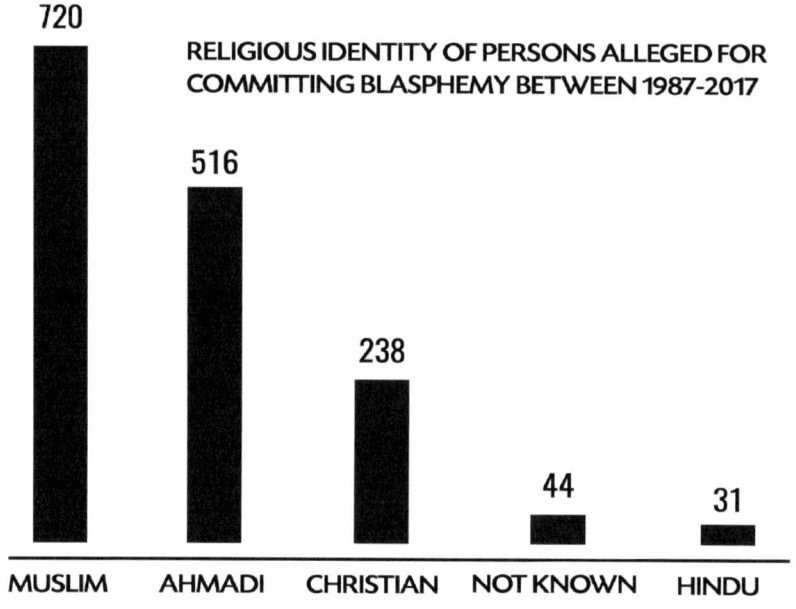

720

RELIGIOUS IDENTITY OF PERSONS ALLEGED FOR COMMITTING BLASPHEMY BETWEEN 1987-2017

516

238

44

31

MUSLIM   AHMADI   CHRISTIAN   NOT KNOWN   HINDU

**Asiya bibi case** is also a big example of misuse of blasphemy laws in Pakistan where Pakistani Christian woman, Aasia, who was convicted of blasphemy by a Pakistani court, receiving a sentence of death by hanging.[30] In _**Ayub Masih v The State**_, the SC observed that the complainant wanted to seize the land of Ayub Masih and his father, after involving them in a

29 Mohammad Nafees, "Blasphemy laws in Pakistan: A historical overview", Centre for Research and Security Studies, Islamabad, 2013, p. 44, available at www.csi-int.org/fileadmin/Files/pdf/2014/blasphemylawsinpakistan.pdf

30 Mst **Asia Bibi** v The State

false blasphemy case.[31] In short, these laws promote nothing but hatred against other religions and it led to an increase in communal and sectarian violence in the society.

ii. Extra judicial killings

The supporter of 295-C said that death penalty discourages people to take law into their hands. During the British Raj, only two people accused of blasphemy, were extra judicially murdered.[32] After the creation of Pakistan and enactment of these additional blasphemy laws, the number of extrajudicial killings has now gone up to **59** people, including judges, governor, clerics women, children and men.[33] Despite having so many different blasphemy laws in the country, state is unable to ensure that people resort to legal means instead of taking the law into their own hands and commit crime of killing an alleged blasphemer extra-judicially. The ATC decision in the case of **_Salman Taseer's_** murder can be a good source of guidance.[34] It states that a person who is leading a sinful life be termed an apostate? Secondly, if he is deemed an apostate, then who will execute him? Individuals cannot be allowed to execute such persons because it will lead to lawlessness in the society. The entire intention and purpose of having a law for dealing with an offence by using legal means seems to have lost its credibility in Pakistan. Furthermore, extrajudicial murders and rise in blasphemy offenses prove that this law has been grossly misused and this practice needs to stop.

In 2017, A 23-year-old student, **_MASHAL KHAN_**, of Abdul Wali Khan University, Mardan, was killed as he was blamed for publishing blasphemous content online. [35]

iii. Discrimination on the basis of religion

---

31 PLD 2002 SC 1048.

32 Nafees, Mohammad. "Blasphemy Laws in Pakistan A Historical Overview."

33 Islamic Shariah and Blasphemy Laws in Pakistan. *The Round Table by Shakir*

34 Raja, Mudassir. "Verdict Is In: Death Penalty for Taseer's Assassin." The Express Tribune Verdict Is in Death Penalty for Taseers Assassin Comments. The Express Tribune

35 https://bolojawan.com/verdict-of-mashal-khan-murder-case/

Article 25 of the Constitution of Pakistan states that all are equal before the law[36] but on the other hand section 295-C discriminate people on the basis of their religion. This section does not protect anti-religion speech but it protects only anti-Islam speech. It can implied that this law have given right to every Muslim to insult or abuse any other religion but when any minority say something back to the Islam it considers as blasphemy. Section 295-C is also in violation with **Article 14** of the constitution which talks about the dignity of man.[37] Speaking against some religious minority's belief necessarily humiliates that minority and also it violated the human dignity.

Part V: ISLAMIC CRITIQUE

It has been said that the blasphemy law is based on Islamic principles of sharia. Even If we analyze these laws according to standards of sharia even then these laws appears unjust. Even though there are several instances of blasphemy committed by infidels against Holy Prophet PBUH but Holy Prophet PBUH always forgave their enemies.

And when they hear vain talk, they turn away therefrom and say: "to us our deeds and to
you yours; peace be to you." [Quran 28: 55][38]

Verse 141 of Chapter 4 of Holy Quran states that when you hear the Signs of Allah being denied and mocked at, sit not with them until they engage in a talk other than that; for in that case you would be like them. [39]

It is clear that instead of punishing the blasphemers, Muslims are directed to leave the company of Blasphemers until they change the topic of their discussion.[40] The concept of

---

36 Article: 25 Equality of citizens.

37 Article 14: Inviolability of dignity of man, etc

38 Quran 28: 55

39 Quran 4: 141

40 The Salman Rushdie Affair: Apostasy, Honor, and Freedom of Speech 1993

blasphemy and the prescribed punishment in Penal Code of Pakistan are both contradictory to the Qur'an and the Prophet's conduct.

Part VI: RECOMMENDATIONS

Blasphemy laws have been the most controversial laws in the history of Pakistan. This paper will discuss some recommendations which will make this section better and likely to not to misuse. By looking at empirical data it can be evidently seen that the harsh punishments introduced by general Zia ul Haq increased the number of complaints and add into the problems.

- Compulsory *death sentence* is in violation with the fundamental right to life which is guaranteed in our constitution. The punishment should be reduced to a maximum five years.
- Secondly the element of <u>intention</u> must be introduced into the section 295-C by adding words like by adding words maliciously, deliberately and intentionally.

This section is badly drafted and wording is too vague. There is a need to clear the wording of this section by redrafting so that it will further reduce chances of misuse.

CONCLUSION

Section 295-C resulted in the unjust persecution, imprisonment and even the death of innocent people. The attachment of Islam with these so called Islamic laws is agonizing for many Muslims. There are several flaws in blasphemy laws of Pakistan and these laws are frequently misused in criminal justice system. It is also worth mentioning that even Islamic principles does not allow for such discriminatory and unjust laws. Therefore it can be suggested that the punishment should be reduced and the text of the laws should be reviewed so there is no room left for any kind of misinterpretation. Faiz once said;

مٹ جائے گی مخلوق تو انصاف کرو گے

منصف ہو تو اب حشر اُٹھا کیوں نہیں دیتے

Works Cited

i. Ahmed, Rabia. "What Happened to 'Innocent until Proven Guilty'?" *Pakistan Today*, www.pakistantoday.com.pk/2017/11/27/what-happened-to-innocent-until-proven-guilty/.

ii. Apostasy, et al. "What Is the Punishment for Blasphemy in Islam?" *Review of Religions*, 21 June 2019, www.reviewofreligions.org/5002/what-is-the-punishment-for-blasphemy-in-islam/.

iii. *Blasphemy Laws in Pakistan: a Historical Overview*. Center for Research and Security Studies, 2013.

iv. Bosch, Miriam Díez, and Jordi Sánchez Torrents. *On Blasphemy*. Facultat De Comunicació i Relacions Internacionals Blanquerna, Universitat Ramon Llull, 2015.

v. "The Constitution of Pakistan, 1973 Developed by Zain Sheikh." *The Constitution of Pakistan, 1973 Developed by Zain Sheikh*, pakistanconstitutionlaw.com/.

vi. Euronews, and Euronews. "Pakistan 'Blasphemy Killing': Murdered Student 'Devoted to Islam'." *Euronews*, 14 Apr. 2017, www.euronews.com/2017/04/14/pakistan-blasphemy-killing-murdered-student-devoted-to-islam.

vii. Hewett, Bob. *The Book of Blasphemy*. Authors OnLine, 2002.

viii. Jackson, Wayne. "Blasphemy - What Is This Great Sin?" *Christian Courier*, www.christiancourier.com/articles/168-blasphemy-what-is-this-great-sin.

ix. Khan, Dr.Zeeshan. "Freedom of Speech and Blasphemy." *The Nation*, The Nation, 27

Sept. 2018, nation.com.pk/28-Sep-2018/freedom-of-speech-and-blasphemy.

x. Khan, M Ilyas. "Asia Bibi: Pakistan Supreme Court's 'Historic' Ruling." *BBC News*, BBC, 31 Oct. 2018, www.bbc.com/news/world-asia-46048134.

xi. McCarthy, Rory. "Blasphemy Doctor Faces Death." *The Guardian*, Guardian News and Media, 20 Aug. 2001, www.theguardian.com/world/2001/aug/20/rorymccarthy.

xii. "PAKISTAN: Another Person Sentenced to Death under Blasphemy Law." *Asian Human Rights Commission*, www.humanrights.asia/news/urgent-appeals/UA-35-2002/.

xiii. Press Trust of India. "No Evidence, No Witness: Pak Supreme Court Releases Man After 18 Years." *NDTV.com*, 26 Sept. 2019, www.ndtv.com/world-news/pakistan-supreme-court-releases-man-sentenced-to-death-after-18-years-says-no-evidence-no-witness-2107600.

xiv. Shakir, Naeem. "Islamic Shariah and Blasphemy Laws in Pakistan." *The Round Table*, vol. 104, no. 3, 2015, pp. 307–317., doi:10.1080/00358533.2015.1053235.

xv. Siddique, et al. "Unholy Speech and Holy Laws: Blasphemy Laws in Pakistan – Controversial Origins, Design Defects and Free Speech Implications." *SSRN*, 26 Jan. 2013, papers.ssrn.com/sol3/papers.cfm?abstract_id=2207002.

xvi. Slaughter, M. M. "The Salman Rushdie Affair: Apostasy, Honor, and Freedom of Speech." *Virginia Law Review*, vol. 79, no. 1, 1993, p. 153., doi:10.2307/1073409.

xvii. United Nations. "Use and Abuse of the Blasphemy Laws." *Refworld*, www.refworld.org/docid/3ae6a9aa4.html.

xviii. "Where Did the Blasphemy Law Come from?" *Blogs*, blogs.tribune.com.pk/story/3270/where-did-the-blasphemy-law-come-from/.

YOUR KNOWLEDGE HAS VALUE

- We will publish your bachelor's and
  master's thesis, essays and papers

- Your own eBook and book -
  sold worldwide in all relevant shops

- Earn money with each sale

Upload your text at www.GRIN.com
and publish for free